The BFG

Sophie invites her father to play the BFG

From L to R: David Burrows (Daniel), Adam Stafford (Sam), Joesephine Baird (Rebecca), Janet Cost-Chrétien (Katherine), Mary-Ann Coburn (Mother), Adrian Phillips (Guy), Anthony Pedley (Father) and Fiona Grogan (Sophie)

The BFG
(Big Friendly Giant)
by Roald Dahl

Adapted for the stage by
David Wood

Samuel French - London
New York - Toronto - Hollywood

THE BFG

The BFG snatches Sophie from the orphanage   *From L to R:* Anthony Pedley (BFG) and Fiona Grogan (Sophie)

THE BFG

The BFG was first performed at Wimbledon Theatre on 19th February, 1991 and on tour, followed by a West End season for Christmas at the Aldwych Theatre. The play was presented by James Woods and Justin Savage for Clarion Productions, and Robert Cogo-Fawcett for Lyric Hammersmith Productions, by arrangement with Theatre Royal Presentations plc, with the following cast:

Actor 1 **Anthony Pedley**
Actor 2 **Mary-Ann Coburn**
Actor 3 **Fiona Grogan**
Actor 4 **Adrian Phillips**
Actor 5 **David Burrows**
Actor 6 **Adam Stafford**
Actor 7 **Janet Cost-Chrétien**
Actor 8 **Josephine Baird**

Director **David Wood**
Associate Director **Ben Forster**
Designer **Susie Caulcutt**
Lighting designer **Simon Courtenay-Taylor**
Movement **Sheila Falconer**
Music composer and supervisor **Peter Pontzen**
Musical director **Cliff Atkinson**
Puppetry consultant **Paul Aylett**
Sound designer **Mark Furness**

Cast of characters with suggested doubling

Actor 1   Dad/the BFG

Actor 2   Mum/Childchewer/Miss Plumridge/the Queen
of England

Actor 3   Sophie

Actor 4   Guy (Sophie's brother)/Fleshlumpeater/Head-
teacher/Mr Tibbs

Actor 5   Daniel (Sophie's friend)/Bloodbottler/Class-
mate/Ronald Simkins/Head of the Army

Actor 6   Sam (Sophie's friend)/Bonecruncher/Class-
mate/Sam Simkins/Head of the Air Force

Actor 7   Katherine (Sophie's friend)/Meatdripper/Class-
mate/Mary

Actor 8   Rebecca   (Sophie's   friend)/Gizzardgulper/
Rebecca (dreamer)/Undermaid/Queen of
Sweden

All the cast help set the scenes and act as puppeteers

The action of the play starts in Sophie's attic playroom/
bedroom and moves to the BFG's cave in Giant
Country; Dream Country and Buckingham Palace.

ACKNOWLEDGEMENTS

Photographs
The photographs in this Acting Edition are from the original production and are reproduced by permission of the photographer, Donald Cooper.

Headdress designs
The original headdress designs for the Giants are reproduced on pages 40–45 by kind permission of the designer, Susie Caulcutt.

Music
Optional incidental music, composed by Peter Pontzen for the original production, is available from Samuel French Ltd.

INTRODUCTION

The BFG is a very popular and deeply loved children's book about a twenty-four-feet-high giant and a little girl—not perhaps the most obvious subject for faithful stage adaptation.

But, in the knowledge that if children themselves, in a playtime situation, wished to act out the story of *The BFG*, they would undoubtedly find an imaginative and convincing way, I decided to use that very knowledge and have a family and friends act out the story at a birthday party as a "play within a play".

Thus, using as props objects in a playroom such as puppets, a dolls' house or a fishing net, the actors could tell the tale in an apparently improvisatory manner.

Yet this device, I felt, was not enough. It was fine for the Giant Country scenes, in which the giants could be played by human beings and the only human character (Sophie) could be played by a puppet, thus offering an effective sense of scale. But the scenes in England are mostly populated by human beings, who needed to be played by human beings, thus necessitating the Giant to be played by a giant puppet; this change of scale was, I thought, satisfyingly theatrical and offered the possibility of developing the fantasy of the "improvised" beginning into a more naturalistic presentation of the later scenes, even to the extent of introducing a complete transformation scene change as the world of the imagination took over.

By a sad coincidence, Mr Roald Dahl died while this play was being written. It is dedicated to him with great respect and admiration.

David Wood

The Giants

From L to R: Adrian Phillips, Janet Cost-Chrétien, Adam Stafford, Josephine Baird, Mary-Ann Coburn, David Burrows

Fleshlumpeater: "You is not switchfiddling us, is you?"

From L to R: David Burrows (Fleshlumpeater), Adam Stafford (Bloodbottler) Anthony Pedley (BFG)

Notes on some of the trickier props

"Sophie" doll This should be a doll version of Sophie in her nightdress, wearing glasses. It is really a puppet and could have a central rod with which to hold it and turn the head. Another rod could be attached to one wrist to give arm mobility. The suggested height is 15–18 inches; this both gives visibility and offers enough contrast in size between it and the BFG actor. Incidentally, in the original production the BFG found it most convenient to carry the "Sophie" doll, when travelling, by inserting the puppet rod in his belt, on his left hip, then covering it with his cloak.

BFG suitcase This should accommodate three dream jars (without rattling). Clips alongside the handle should accommodate the horn/trumpet, because the BFG needs to carry the suitcase *and* the horn/trumpet safely in one hand.

The Giants' headdresses Rather than masks, which tend to muffle and distort actors' voices, large helmets are suggested, on top of which the giants' heads sit. The actors' faces are therefore visible, but not very noticeable if they lower their heads a little. Designs from the original production are on pages 41–45.

Snozzcumbers Several are required, to resemble oversize, knobbly cucumbers. One should split in two, possibly using "velcro", revealing the fleshy, pip-filled inside. The "Sophie" doll, when hiding, need not literally slip inside the snozzcumber; if slid *behind* it, the necessary illusion can be created.

Frobscottle A large green bottle with a removable stopper. It need not pour real liquid. In the original production, a battery-operated light and revolving mechanism inside created the illusion of "downward bubbles".

Dream jars Most of the jars on the shelves in the cave can be fixed and wired with flickering lights or fibre optics. But the ones the BFG uses to catch dreams in the Dream Country scene need to have a battery-operated device whereby, when stoppered, they gradually glow in an appropriate colour.

Queen's early-morning tea tray This has to be dropped (without breaking the crockery every performance!), but, also, the crockery and teapot need to rattle. It is suggested that items are partially attached to the tray, through a white tray cloth, and that the cup is "velcro'd" to the saucer, to allow it to be dislodged without breaking.

Giant BFG head This appears at the window and can be a large cut-out on a pole, operated by a stage manager, or a more sophisticated puppet-head.

Giant BFG puppet Sitting on a piano and chest of drawers, as in the familiar picture in the original book, this puppet could be operated from inside, or manipulated in vision from outside. The larger the better! And, obviously, the more it resembles the actor playing the BFG, the better. Many people thought the puppet in the original production was "animatronic", because it had head and mouth movements, plus arm movements and even leg movements (during whizzpopping!); but all these apparent sophistications were achieved by straight-forward puppetry, and operated by the BFG actor inside.

Rod puppets These are small versions of the Queen of England, Mr Tibbs, the Head of the Army, the Head of the Air Force, Mary and the Undermaid. They should be in scale with the "Sophie" doll, and operated by two rods, one central and the other attached to the wrist to enable the puppets to wave at the end.

Shadow puppets Operated on rods, these need a suitable screen and an appropriate light source from behind. In the original production the screen was a "front cloth" behind which the attic/bedroom could be re-set during the shadow puppet sequence.

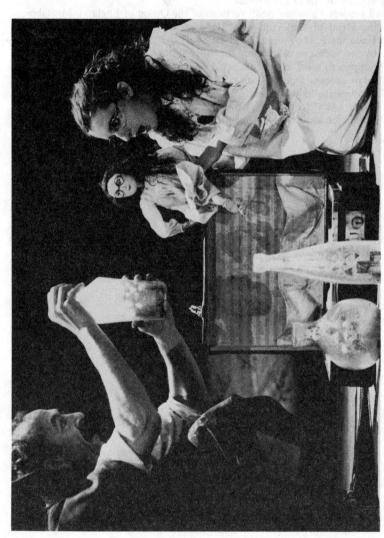

The BFG shows Sophie a dream   *From L to R*: Anthony Pedley (BFG) and Fiona Grogan (Sophie)

The Queen: "We have a job for you."
From L to R: Fiona Grogan (Sophie), Mary-Ann Coburn (Queen of England),
David Burrows (Head of Army), Adam Stafford (Head of Air Force)

ACT I

Sophie's attic playroom/bedroom

This is an exciting space with colourful toys and books on shelves, a rocking horse, a dolls' house, a toy grand piano, musical instruments including a trumpet/horn, a fishing net, a puppet booth, toy helicopters, a suitcase, a dressing-up chest, plus a rail of dressing-up clothes and masks, wigs, crown, etc. and cuddly toys. There is also a chest of drawers, a grandfather clock, Sophie's bed, a door to the landing and perhaps a door to a cupboard. A major feature of the room is a large studio window with curtains, in front of which is a platform, which can be used as a thrust stage. Small staircases lead up to it. Chairs have been placed to one side to give space for Sophie's birthday party

As the Curtain rises this is in full swing. A banner proclaims "Happy Birthday, Sophie". Hastily unwrapped presents lie around

Sophie and her friends, Daniel, Katherine, Rebecca and Sam are playing blind man's buff. Daniel is blindfolded and advances, arms outstretched, towards the others, who circle him. They giggle and shriek as he makes a few near-miss grabs. Eventually he grabs Sophie, who screams with delight

Daniel Gotcha! Now who have we got here?
Sophie (*in a deep voice*) It's me. Sam!

Laughter

Daniel No it's not. It's ... Sophie!

Laughter and applause. Daniel takes off the blindfold

Sophie Very good Danny. Now, let's play Grandmother's Footsteps!
Rebecca Bags be Grandmother.
Sophie Right. Becky's Grandmother.

Rebecca turns her back as the others stand in a line

Rebecca Ready.
Sam No peeping.

They advance on tiptoe. Rebecca suddenly turns, but can't catch anyone moving. Another go. This time she catches Danny moving

Rebecca Danny.

Danny goes back to the "start". Rebecca turns her back again. All advance towards her. Katherine rushes to Rebecca and taps her on the back

(*With a jump*) Katherine!

Katherine OK. My turn.

She takes Rebecca's place. The others go back in line and the game starts again

Suddenly loud, booming footsteps echo from outside

All freeze in fright

Katherine What's that?
Daniel A very fat Grandmother!

They laugh nervously

Suddenly a voice booms from outside

Guy (*off*) Fee, fi, fo, fum. I'm coming to gobble you up!

The children scream and cluster in a group watching the door, which bursts open

   Guy enters

Guy It's only me! Fooled you!
Sophie Guy! It's Guy, everyone, my boring big brother.

All relax

Guy Hi, everyone. Happy birthday, Sophie.

He produces a present from behind his back

Sophie (*opening it*) Thanks. (*Finding a book: The BFG*) Hey! *The BFG*! My favourite book! I've borrowed it from the library three times!
Guy You've got your very own copy now!
Rebecca What's it about?
Sophie A huge giant.
Guy (*advancing on the group*) Fee, fi, fo, fum!
Sophie Shut up, Guy. And thanks!

   Mum and Dad enter, rather flustered

Mum Hallo, everyone.
All Hallo.
Sophie Look what Guy's given me, Mum.
Mum (*not really noticing*) Lovely, Sophie. Now, listen, everyone. I don't know quite how to tell you, but . . .
Dad You see, for Sophie's party we booked an entertainer . . .

The children cheer

   No, no, listen. He's just phoned to say he's very sorry but he's been taken ill. A tummy bug or something.
Mum So . . . no entertainer. Sorry, folks.

Silence

Guy Oh, come on, kids, it's not that bad. We'll just have to make our *own* entertainment.
Sophie (*suddenly*) I know! We'll do *The BFG*!
Dad Do the what?
Sophie Tell the story. Act it out! Please! We've got the dressing-up box. I'll be Sophie, the girl in the story. (*To the children*) You can all be giants. Guy can be Fleshlumpeater.

The children all rush excitedly to the dressing-up box

Dad Well, that's settled then. Have fun!

He and Mum start to go

Sophie (*stopping him*) Dad, you can't go. You're the BFG!
Dad Me?
Sophie You. And there's a great part for Mum later.
Mum Really?
Dad All right, then.

The children cheer

We'd better get ready.

Mum and Dad join the children preparing, finding props and bits of costume. Sophie finds her nightie under her pillow, plus a "Sophie" doll

Sophie (*putting her nightie on over her other clothes*) Stand by, everyone. Music! Lights!

One of the children tinkles on the toy grand piano. Eventually the musical director takes over. Another child lowers the lights

(*Announcing*) The BFG!

Holding a toy trumpet, one of the children sounds a loud fanfare

(*Starting the story*) It was late at night . . .

Someone makes an owl hooting noise

. . . in the orphanage.

Sophie looks around and sees the dolls' house. She motions to Guy, who places it in a prominent position. From now on, the cast 'make the story happen', improvising props, setting up scenes and also acting as an audience

In the dormitory, Sophie couldn't sleep. (*She opens the dolls' house and places the "Sophie" doll inside*) A brilliant moonbeam was shining right on to her pillow.

Someone shines a torch on the dolls' house

She slipped out of bed to get a drink of water.
Mum (*a voice from the darkness*) Sophie! Back to bed this instant. You know the rules.

Sophie Mrs Clonkers. Sophie went back to bed. She tried very hard to doze off. The time ticked by. The house was absolutely silent. Perhaps, thought Sophie, this is what they call the witching hour, that special moment in the middle of the night when everyone is in a deep, deep sleep, and all the dark things come out from hiding and have the world to themselves. She crept to the window. And suddenly she saw . . . a giant!

Sinister music as Dad, in a cloak and carrying a suitcase, appears as the BFG. He looms over the dolls' house, then proceeds to another part of the room, acting out the narration

He stopped at the house opposite, bent down to look in a bedroom window and then . . .

The BFG opens his suitcase, takes out a jar and pours its contents into the end of a horn-like trumpet. Then he blows through it into the imaginary window. He replaces the jar and trumpet in his case. He turns towards the dolls' house

(*With a gasp*) He saw Sophie. She pulled back from the window, flew across the dormitory and jumped into her bed and hid under the blanket, tingling all over.

The BFG approaches the dolls' house as the music intensifies. He peeps in the window, and, with a growl, pushes his hand through the window and snatches the "Sophie" doll

Aaaaaaaah!

The BFG tucks the "Sophie" doll inside his cloak and goes up on to the platform stage

The curtains are drawn, revealing the window. The area is suddenly filled with back light, in which the BFG begins slow-motion, on-the-spot, running

A howling wind blows

Actors Running, striding, leaping through the night. Over fields, over hedges, over rivers, each stride as long as a tennis court. Faster, faster, feet scarcely touching the ground. Over oceans, over forests, over mountains. To a land unknown to human beings.

The BFG slows down and walks off the platform stage. The curtains close and the lighting fades

Sophie swings round a wall of bookshelves or a wardrobe to reveal the BFG's cave with a rough-hewn table and stool and shelves covered with a sack-cloth curtain

The BFG enters the cave, puts down his suitcase, removes his cloak, then carefully brings out the "Sophie" doll. He puts it on the table

Sophie enters the scene and manipulates the doll like a puppet, while providing Sophie's voice

BFG Ha! What has us got here?

He looks carefully at Sophie. At first he should not appear to be very friendly

Sophie (*nervously*) Where am I?
BFG This is my cave.
Sophie Why did you snatch me and bring me here?
BFG Because you *saw* me. If anyone is ever *seeing* a giant, he or she must be taken away hipswitch.
Sophie Why?
BFG Human beans is not believing in giants, is they? Human beans is not thinking giants exist. ××× ⇁
Sophie I do.
BFG Ah, but that is because you has *seen* me. If I hadn't snitched you, you would be scuddling around yodelling the news on the telly-telly bunkum box that you were actually *seeing* a giant, and then a great giant-hunt, a mighty giant look-see would be starting up all over the world, and human beans would be trying to catch me and put me in the zoo with all those squiggling hippodumplings and crocadowndillies.
Sophie So what's going to happen to me now?
BFG You will just have to be staying here with me for the rest of your life.
Sophie Oh no!
BFG Oh yes! Now, I is hungry!
Sophie (*gasping*) Please don't eat *me*!
BFG (*bellowing with laughter*) Just because I is a giant, you think I is a man-gobbling cannybull! No!
Sophie Oh, good.
BFG Yes, you is lucky. If one of the *other* giants is snitching you, they is crunching you up for sure. In one scrumdiddlyumptious mouthful. Bones crackety-crackety-cracking. Gobble, gobbledy, gone!
Sophie Other giants? You mean there are more of you?
BFG Of course! This is Giant Country! (*He picks up the "Sophie" doll*) Be peeping out over there, little girl, and be seeing a brain-bogglingsome sight.

He carries her to the cave entrance

Lights come up on the platform stage, where the other giants appear (Mum, Guy, Katherine, Daniel, Rebecca and Sam wearing giant headdresses)

The giants lumber about, looking menacing and hungry, grunting and occasionally threatening one another. They make themselves identifiable as the BFG mentions them

Sophie Gosh!
BFG Is you believing your gogglers?
Sophie What on earth are they doing?
BFG Nothing. They is just moocheling and footcheling around and waiting for the night to come. Then they will be galloping off to places where human beans is living to find their suppers.
Sophie Where?
BFG All over the world.

Bonecruncher I is fancying a gallop to Turkey to guzzle some tasty Turks.

BFG That's the Bonecruncher. He is thinking Turkish human beans is juiciest beans. They is tasting of . . .

Sophie Turkey?

BFG No! Turkish delight!

Sophie Of course. Who's that big, fierce one?

BFG That's the Fleshlumpeater.

Fleshlumpeater I is fancying getting my chompers round a handful of human beans from Wellington!

Sophie Where's Wellington?

BFG Your head is full of squashed flies. Wellington is in New Zealand.

Sophie What do people in Wellington taste of?

BFG Boots, of course.

Sophie But boots taste horrid.

BFG Rubbsquash! Boots taste bootiful!

Sophie Ha ha.

Bloodbottler I could be murdering some human beans from England!

Sophie England?

BFG That's the Bloodbottler. He is thinking the English is tasting ever so wonderfully of crodscollop.

Sophie I'm not sure I know what that means.

BFG Meanings is not important. I cannot be right all the time. Quite often I is left instead of right.

A row breaks out among the giants. They grunt and push, arguing about where to go

Let's go back. You will be coming to an ucky-mucky end if any of them should ever be getting his gogglers upon you. You would be swallowed up like a piece of frumpkin pie, all in one dollop.

They return inside the cave

The Lights dim on the giants and they exit

There. You is safe in here.

Sophie I think eating people is horrible.

BFG I has told you. *I* is not eating people. Not I! I is a freaky giant! I is a nice and jumbly giant! I is the BFG!

Sophie The BFG?

BFG The Big Friendly Giant! What is *your* name?

Sophie My name is Sophie.

BFG How is you doing, Sophie? (*He shakes hands with the doll*) Is you quite snuggly in your nightie, Sophie? You isn't fridgy cold?

Sophie I'm fine.

BFG I cannot help thinking about your poor mother and father. By now they must be jipping and skumping all over the house shouting, "Hallo, hallo, where is Sophie gone?"

Sophie I don't have a mother and father. They died when I was a baby.

BFG You is a norphan?

Sophie Yes.

BFG Oh you poor little scrumplet. You is making me sad.

Sophie Don't be sad. No-one at the orphanage will be worrying much about me.

BFG Was you happy there?

Sophie I hated it. Mrs Clonkers locked me in the cellar once.

BFG Why?

Sophie For not folding up my clothes.

BFG The rotten old rotrasper!

Sophie It was horrid. There were rats down there.

BFG The filthy old fizzwiggler! You is making me sadder than ever. (*He sobs*)

Sophie Don't cry, BFG. Please. Listen, tell me—if you don't eat humans, what *do* you eat?

BFG (*pulling himself together*) That, little Sophie, is a squelching tricky problem. In this sloshflunking Giant country, happy eats like pineapples and pigwinkles is simply not growing. Nothing is growing except for one extremely icky-poo vegetable. It is called the snozzcumber. →

Sophie The snozzcumber? There's no such thing.

BFG Is you calling me a fibster?

Sophie Well ...

BFG (*getting cross*) Just because you has not *seen* something isn't meaning it isn't existing. What about the great squizzly scotch-hopper?

Sophie I beg your pardon?

BFG And the humplecrimp?

Sophie What's that?

BFG And the wraprascal? And the crumpscoddle?

Sophie Are they animals?

BFG They is *common* animals. Swipe my swoggles! I is not a very know-all giant myself, but it seems to me you is an absolutely know-nothing human bean. Your brain is full of rotten-wool.

Sophie You mean cotton-wool.

BFG (*grandly*) What I mean and what I say is two different things. (*He stands*) I will now show you the repulsant snozzcumber.

The BFG finds a huge black and white striped, knobbly, cucumber-shaped vegetable, rather like a giant's club

Sophie Gosh. It doesn't look very tasty.

BFG It's disgusterous! It's sickable! It's maggot-wise! (*He breaks it in two*) Try some.

Sophie Pooh! No, thank you.

BFG There's nothing else to guzzle. Have a go.

The "Sophie" doll nibbles some

Sophie Uggggh! Oh no! It tastes of frogskins. And rotten fish.

BFG (*roaring with laughter*) Worse than that! To me it is tasting of clockcoaches and slimewanglers.

Sophie Do I really have to eat it?

BFG Unless you is wanting to become so thin you will be disappearing into a thick ear.

Sophie Into *thin air*. A thick ear is something quite different.

BFG (*going to answer back, but checking himself*) Words is oh such a twitch-tickling problem to me. I know exactly what words I is wanting to say, but somehow they come out all squiff-squiddly.

Sophie That happens to everyone.

BFG (*sadly*) Not like it happens to me. I is speaking the most terrible wigglish.

Sophie I think you speak beautifully.

BFG (*brightening*) You do? You is not twiddling my leg?

Sophie No. I love the way you talk.

BFG How wondercrump. How whoopsey-splunkers. Thank you, Sophie.

Sudden thumping and shouting interrupts them

Bloodbottler (*off*) Runt! Runt?

Fleshlumpeater (*off*) What is you up to, runt?

BFG Quick, Sophie, hide.

Sophie (*narrating, as she hides the "Sophie" doll behind the snozzcumber on the table*) Sophie hid behind the snozzcumber.

Bloodbottler and Fleshlumpeater enter

Bloodbottler Aha!

Fleshlumpeater Aha!

They stand threateningly above the BFG, who sits at the table trying to look calm

BFG Hallo, Bloodbottler. Good day, Fleshlumpeater.

Bloodbottler Don't hallo good day us, runt.

Fleshlumpeater We is hearing you jabbeling.

Bloodbottler
Fleshlumpeater } (*together*) Who is you jabbeling to, runt?

BFG I is jabbeling to myself.

Bloodbottler Pifflefizz!

Fleshlumpeater
Bloodbottler } (*together*) You is talking to a human bean!

BFG No, no!

Bloodbottler Yus!

Fleshlumpeater Yus!

Bloodbottler We is guessing you has snitched away a human bean and brought it back to your bunghole as a pet!

Fleshlumpeater So now we is winkling it out and guzzling it as extra snacks before supper!

They start sniffing and searching. The BFG tries to conceal Sophie

BFG (*nervously*) There's no one here. Why don't you leave me alone?

Bloodbottler (*threateningly*) Piffling little swishfiggler!

Fleshlumpeater Squimpy little pogswizzler!

Bloodbottler }
Fleshlumpeater } *(together; sniffing and searching)* Where is it? Where is it?

They freeze

Sophie *(narrating, and manipulating the doll)* Terrified, Sophie scooped out some slimy snozzcumber seeds and, unseen by the BFG, crawled inside the pongy vegetable.

Bloodbottler and Fleshlumpeater see the snozzcumber

Bloodbottler So this is the filthing rotsome clubbage you is eating!

Fleshlumpeater You must be cockles to be guzzling such rubbsquash!

BFG Snozzcumbers is scrumdiddlyumptious.

Bloodbottler Human beans is juicier.

BFG Try some. It's glumptious.

Fleshlumpeater You is not switchfiddling us, is you?

BFG Never. Vegitibbles is very good for you.

Bloodbottler Mmm. Just this once we is going to taste these rotsome eats of yours.

Fleshlumpeater But if it is filthsome, we is smashing it over your sludgy little head!

They each pick up half the snozzcumber. Music as the action goes into slow-motion

Sophie *(narrating)* Sophie felt herself being lifted up and up and up. She clung on desperately to stop herself falling out.

Bloodbottler and Fleshlumpeater mime taking a bite

Suddenly there was a crunch as the Bloodbottler bit a huge hunk off the end. Sophie saw his yellow teeth clamping together. Then, utter darkness. She was in his mouth. Terrified, she waited for the next crunch ...

In slow motion, Bloodbottler and Fleshlumpeater splutter with the horrible taste

Bloodbottler Eeeeeowtch!

Fleshlumpeater Ughbwelch!

They spit

Sophie *(narrating)* All the great lumps of snozzcumber, as well as Sophie herself, went shooting out across the cave.

She manipulates the "Sophie" doll, slowly wheeling it in an arc from the Bloodbottler's mouth to the floor

Bloodbottler and Fleshlumpeater snap out of slow-motion

Bloodbottler You little swinebuggler!

Fleshlumpeater You little pigswiller!

Bloodbottler } (*together*) It's disgusterous!
Fleshlumpeater

They hit the BFG on the head with the snozzcumber halves

BFG (*rubbing his head*) You is not loving it?
Bloodbottler You must be buggles to be swalloping slutch like that!
Fleshlumpeater Every night you could be galloping off happy as a hamburger and gobbling juicy human beans.
BFG Eating human beans is wrong and evil! You is revoltant!
Bloodbottler And you is an insult to the giant peoples! You is not fit to be a giant!
Fleshlumpeater You is a pibbling little pitsqueak! You is a ... a ... a cream puffnut!

Bloodbottler and Fleshlumpeater exit, bellowing

The BFG checks they have gone

BFG (*whispering*) Sophie? Where is you, Sophie?
Sophie I'm here.

The BFG finds the "Sophie" doll on the floor and tenderly picks her up

BFG Oh, I is so happy to be finding you all in one lump.
Sophie I was in the Bloodbottler's mouth!
BFG What?
Sophie I hid in the snozzcumber.
BFG And I was telling him to eat it! You poor little chiddler, forgive me. Oho! You is needing some frobscottle to make you better.

He brings the "Sophie" doll to the table

Sophie Frobscottle?
BFG Frobscottle. (*He proudly finds a bottle of green liquid*) I drink it lots. Delumptious, fizzy frobscottle!

He removes the stopper. There is a fizzing sound. Bubbles are seen going downwards

Sophie Hey, look! It's fizzing the wrong way!
BFG What is you meaning?
Sophie Downwards. In our fizzy drinks, like Coke and Pepsi, the bubbles go upwards.
BFG Flushbunking rubbsquash!
Sophie They do!
BFG Upwards is the wrong way.
Sophie Why?
BFG If you is not seeing why, you must be as quacky as a duckhound! Upgoing bubbles is a catasterous disastrophe.
Sophie But why?
BFG Listen. When you is drinking this cokey drink of yours, it is going straight down into your tummy. Is that right? Or is it left?
Sophie It's right.

BFG And the *bubbles* is going also into your tummy. Right or left?
Sophie Right again.
BFG If the bubbles is fizzing upwards, they will all come swishwiffling up your throat and out of your mouth and make a foulsome belchy burp!
Sophie That's often true. But what's wrong with a little burp now and again? It's sort of fun.
BFG Burping is filthsome. Us giants is never doing it.
Sophie But with *your* drink . . .
BFG Frobscottle.
Sophie With frobscottle, the bubbles in your tummy will be going *downwards* and that could have a far nastier result.
BFG Why nasty?
Sophie Because they'll be coming out somewhere else with an even louder and ruder noise.
BFG A whizzpopper! Us giants is making whizzpoppers all the time! Whizzpopping is a sign of happiness. It is music in our ears!
Sophie But it's . . . it's rude!
BFG But you is whizzpopping, is you not, now and again?
Sophie Everyone is . . . whizzpopping. Kings and queens, film stars, even little babies. But where I come from, it's not polite to talk about it.
BFG Redunculous! If everyone is making whizzpoppers, then why not talk about it? Now, let's be having a swiggle and seeing the result!

The BFG drinks from the bottle. Pause. Then ecstasy fills his face. A very loud whizzpopper nearly shoots him in the air

Whoopee!

And another

Wheeee!

And another

Wheeeeeeee!

Sophie laughs, in spite of herself

Have some yourself.
Sophie Well . . .
BFG Go on. It's gloriumptious!

He holds the bottle to the "Sophie" doll's mouth. Pause

Sophie It's lovely.
BFG Just wait!

Suddenly a whizzpopper propels the "Sophie" doll into the air. Then a succession of whizzpoppers send her somersaulting up and over, over and up

Sophie Wheeee! Wheeeeee!

The BFG roars with laughter

Eventually both settle, the "Sophie" doll in the BFG's arms. Night-time music as the Lights fade

BFG (*yawning*) Time for a snoozy sleep. Good night, Sophie.
Sophie (*sleepily*) That was fun. Goodnight, BFG.

The Lights fade

  Elsewhere, dim lighting fades up on the other giants entering

Fleshlumpeater 'Tis the witchy hour!

The others grunt their agreement and all begin a kind of war-dance. Suddenly they all freeze

Meatdripper 'Tis time for supper!

All excitedly agree and lumber round again. They suddenly stop

Bloodbottler Human beans . . .
All Here we come!

There is a strobe-type lighting effect and exciting music as the giants run towards the audience, pounding along on the spot. Eventually they stop and the Lights change as they menacingly look about them, hungrily sniffing. Suddenly, with a whoop, they swoop on dolls on Sophie's bed, and savagely mime eating them. Having gorged themselves, they happily return to their former positions on the platform stage, and, as though in a drunken stupor, start snoring

Music suggests time passing

The Lights fade down on the giants, then slowly up as dawn breaks in the cave

The BFG wakes, carefully puts the sleeping "Sophie" doll on the table, and moves to his shelves. He quietly draws the sack-cloth curtain, revealing rows and rows of glass jars, all magically flickering with different coloured lights. He puts three empty jars in his suitcase, closes it, then puts on his cloak. He picks up his fishing net and starts to tip-toe from the cave

Suddenly the "Sophie" doll wakes up

Sophie BFG?
BFG (*stopping*) Yes.
Sophie Where are you going?
BFG I is going to work.
Sophie Back where I live? Blowing your trumpet thing?
BFG (*shocked*) You is seeing me blowing?
Sophie Yes. What were you doing?
BFG Is I trusting you?
Sophie Of course.
BFG Well, then. I, Sophie, is a dream-blowing giant. I blows dreams into the bedrooms of sleeping chiddlers. Nice dreams. Lovely golden dreams. Dreams that is giving the dreamers a happy time.
Sophie Gosh.
BFG See these jars? I is keeping the dreams in them.

He carries the "Sophie" doll to look

Sophie These are all dreams? But where do you get them?
BFG I collect them.
Sophie Collect them? That's impossible.
BFG You isn't believing in dreams?
Sophie Well, of course, but . . .
BFG Listen. Dreams is very mysterious things. They is floating around in the air, like wispy misty bubbles, searching for sleeping people. Come on. I is showing you. You is coming dream-collecting with me!
Sophie (*loudly*) Really? Yes, please!
BFG Shhh! Hold your breaths and cross your figglers. Here we go! Y ⅄ ⊐

He tucks the "Sophie" doll in his cloak, and sets off from the cave. The "shelves door" is closed by Sophie, who then observes the action

The Lights come up on the platform stage, where the other giants are still snoring

The BFG creeps past them, treading carefully between their sprawled limbs. Just as we think he has negotiated them:

Fleshlumpeater Ho-ho there, runt!
Bloodbottler Ho-ho there, little grobsquiffler!
BFG (*trying to be casual*) Ho-ho there, has you had a good feasting?

The other giants are waking

Fleshlumpeater We has had a glumptious gorging!
Bloodbottler In Sweden!
Bonecruncher We is liking the Sweden sour taste!

The giants laugh

Fleshlumpeater Where is you going, runty one?

He grabs the BFG (on stage level) from above

Bloodbottler Where is you splatch-winkling away to?

He too grabs the BFG

BFG (*nervously*) Be so kind as to be letting go.

The other giants advance

Bonecruncher Let's be having him!
Fleshlumpeater To you, Bonecruncher!

He pushes him towards Bonecruncher. The giants roughly push him one to another

Bonecruncher To you, Meatdripper!
Meatdripper To you, Gizzardgulper!
Gizzardgulper To you, Childchewer!
Childchewer To you, Bonecruncher!

They laugh as the BFG, feverishly hanging on to his suitcase and fishing net, and, of course, the "Sophie" doll, is shoved to and fro

Sophie (*narrating*) Inside the BFG's cloak, Sophie clung on for dear life. At last the other giants tired of their game.
Fleshlumpeater Run away, little runt!

Stunned, the BFG starts to stagger away

Bloodbottler Troggy little twit!
Bonecruncher Shrivelly little shrimp!
Meatdripper Mucky little midget!
Gizzardgulper Squaggy little squib!
Childchewer Grobby little grub!

Laughing, they retire

The BFG checks the "Sophie" doll is all right under his cloak, then escapes through the door

There is music and the sound of a whistling wind as swirls of mist envelop the stage. Coloured lights glow and dance on the smoke. Eventually:

Sophie (*plus optional offstage echoes; narrating*) The BFG, clutching Sophie tight to his chest, ran and ran, leaped and galloped and flew . . . till at last . . .

The BFG enters through the mist

He takes the "Sophie" doll from his cloak. Sophie takes the doll and manipulates it once more

BFG We is here!
Sophie Where?
BFG We is in Dream Country. Where all dreams is beginning.

Electronic sounds create a mysterious mood

The "Sophie" doll looks on as, to music, the BFG opens his suitcase, then watches, waits, and suddenly spies a floating dream. He slowly advances with his net, takes aim, then, with a swooping motion, leaps in the air and "catches" the dream. Delighted, he transfers the dream to a jar, which lights up with a golden glow as he corks it

Another watchful wait, then a sighting. An energetic chase, at first "missing" the dream, starting again, then triumphantly "catching" it and transferring it to a jar, which glows pink

The "Sophie" doll watches as the BFG waits once more, the colours still swirling against the misty background. A third dream is sighted. Having caught it, the BFG has a struggle as it tries to escape the net. He tames it finally, and transfers it, using all his strength, to a jar, which glows green

> *Placing the jars in the suitcase and snapping it shut, the BFG takes the "Sophie" doll, puts it under his cloak, and disappears through the mist*

There is the sound of a whistling wind, as the Lights change, and Sophie re-opens the "shelves door" to reveal the BFG's cave once more. The jars on his shelves glimmer and glow

Sophie (*narrating*) By the time the BFG and Sophie arrived back at the cave, darkness was beginning to fall.

The BFG enters the cave, puts his suitcase on the table, and carefully takes the "Sophie" doll from under his cloak. Sophie takes her and manipulates her once more, making her stand on the table, watching as the BFG removes his cloak, then opens the suitcase

BFG Let us see what dreams we is catching! (*He holds up the golden jar*) Oh my! It's a phizzwizard! A golden phizzwizard!
Sophie Is that good?
BFG The best. This will be giving some chiddler a very happy night when I is blowing it in.
Sophie How can you tell?
BFG I is hearing the dream's special music. I is understanding it.
Sophie Gosh.
BFG Shall I be showing Sophie this dream?
Sophie Oh, yes please. But how?
BFG Concentratiate. Watch and be listening!

As they stare at the jar, the Lights fade from the cave and come up in another area. But the jar's golden glow continues to shine

On Sophie's bed lies Rebecca, asleep. Suddenly, to eerie music, her head starts to turn from side to side

Rebecca I'm dreaming ... I'm dreaming ... I'm (*She opens her eyes, then gets off the bed. She acts out her dream*) at school ... in class ... and my teacher, Miss Plumridge, is droning on in a very boring way about William the Conqueror and the Battle of Hastings ...

Mum acts the teacher, as though talking to the class and writing on the blackboard. Daniel, Sam and Katherine play other children in class

... when suddenly I can't help myself humming a little tune. (*She hums*)
Mum/Miss Plumridge Rebecca, cease that humming this instant!
Rebecca ... but I can't help myself humming my little tune, and I hum it louder ... (*She hums it louder*)
Mum/Miss Plumridge Rebecca, how *dare* you! I said stop ...

Rebecca 'fluences' Miss Plumridge, who suddenly freezes. The other children have joined in the humming

Rebecca Suddenly she freezes, then slowly but surely she starts to dance!

Mum/Miss Plumridge slowly starts to dance, unsure of what is happening to her. This builds into a wild, uncontrolled rock'n'roll kind of shake, arms flailing, legs kicking. The class hums and "la las" louder, thoroughly enjoying the fun

Suddenly the door opens and the Headmaster (Guy) bursts in

The humming stops but Miss Plumridge goes on dancing

Rebecca The Headmaster!
Guy/Headmaster What's going on in here? (*He sees Miss Plumridge*) Miss Plumridge! How dare you dance in class. Go fetch your coat and leave this school for ever! You are sacked! You are a disgrace!
Rebecca 'fluences' the Headmaster. He freezes as Rebecca starts to hum again. The others join in

Suddenly the Headmaster starts to dance too. Unable to resist, he too starts jigging around, and builds up into a wild explosion of movement. The class enjoy it even more when he starts jiving with Miss Plumridge. Both still look shocked. The class clap in rhythm and join in the dance, still humming and "la la-ing"

During this, Rebecca, returns to bed

Everything reaches a climax, then suddenly stops. All clear to reveal Rebecca on the bed

Katherine/Mummy (*off*) Rebecca!
Rebecca Then suddenly I hear Mummy's voice . . .
Katherine/Mummy (*off*) Wake up! Your breakfast is ready!

Rebecca jolts upright, and looks disappointed, then, remembering her dream, roars with laughter

The Lights fade and come up again in the cave, where the BFG and Sophie gaze at the golden jar, and laugh

Sophie What a funny dream!
BFG It's a ringbeller! A whoppsy!

He places the golden jar on the shelf

Sophie Can we see another one? Please?
BFG We can.

He takes the pink one from the suitcase. They stare at it

Oho! This is a pink dinghummer! Concentratiate! Watch and be listening!

The Lights fade, leaving the pink jar glowing. The Lights come up in another area

Sam lies on the bed. Suddenly, to eerie music, his head starts to turn from side to side

Sam I'm dreaming. . . . I'm dreaming. . . . I'm . . . (*He opens his eyes, then gets out of bed. He acts out his dream*) doing my homework, trying to work out a nasty bit of algebra, when suddenly . . .

A telephone rings and there is a voice from off stage—Father (Daniel)

Daniel/Father (*off*) Sam! Answer that will you?
Sam (*calling*) I'm doing my homework, Dad.
Daniel/Father (*off*) I'm in the bath. Answer it!

Sam (*calling*) You said I had to do my homework, Dad.

A growl from Father, who enters from the platform stage as though coming downstairs. His hair is wet and he is dressed in a bath towel. He is very pompous

Daniel/Father You'll pay for this, Sam. (*He finds the telephone receiver and picks it up. The telephone stops ringing. Fiercely*) Hallo. Simpkins here. (*In amazement*) What . . . who? (*When he hears the reply, he stands to attention and tries to smarten himself up*) Good evening sir. . . . yes, sir, how can I help you, sir?. . . . Simpkins, sir . . . Ronald Simpkins. . . . no, sir, Ronald, how can I help?. . . . Who? . . . Well, yes sir, there *is* a *Sam* Simpkins on this number, but surely it is *me* you wish to speak to, sir, not my little son?. . . . Yes, sir, very well, sir, I will get him, sir. (*Turning to Sam*) Sam, it's for you.

Sam Oh. Who is it, Dad?

Daniel/Father The er . . . the President of the United States.

Sam (*matter of factly*) Oh, right. (*He takes the receiver*)

Daniel/Father (*staggered*) Do you *know* the President of the United States?

Sam (*with a smile*) No, but I expect he's heard of me.

As he speaks on the telephone, Father watches, eyes wide, mouth open in disbelief

(*Casually*) Hallo. . . . Oh hi!. . . . What's the problem?. . . . OK Mr President, leave it to me, I'll take care of it . . . No, no, you'll bungle it all up if you do it your way. . . . A pleasure, Mr President. Now I must get on with my algebra homework! Bye! Have a nice day!

Father watches, bemused as Sam puts down the telephone and returns to lie on the bed, asleep

Father exits

Daniel/Father (*off*) Sam!

Sam Then suddenly I hear Dad's voice.

Daniel/Father (*off*) Get up you lazy slob or you'll be late for school!

Sam jolts upright, and looks disappointed, then, remembering his dream, roars with laughter

The Lights fade and come up again in the cave, where the BFG and Sophie gaze at the pink jar, and laugh

Sophie That was good too!

BFG A dumhinger, I is telling you! (*He places the pink jar on the shelf and then takes the green one from his suitcase*) Now, what has we here? (*He looks at it. Suddenly*) Aaaaaaah!

Sophie What's the matter?

BFG (*in alarm*) Oh no! I is catching . . . a trogglehumper!

Sophie A trogglehumper?

BFG Yes. A bad, bad dream. A nightmare!

Sophie Oh dear. What will you do with that?

BFG I is never blowing it! If I do, then some poor little tottler will be having the most curdbloodling time! (*He puts it in his suitcase*) I is taking it back tomorrow. (*With a shudder*) Uggh! I is hating trogglehumpers.

Suddenly a roar startles them, the roar of the other giants

Quick! Let's go look-see!

As he and the "Sophie" doll go to the cave entrance, the Lights crossfade to the platform stage, where the other giants assemble, with energy and evil intent

Bloodbottler 'Tis the witchy hour. And I is starveling!
Fleshlumpeater I is starveling rotten too!
Giants And I! And I! And I!
Bonecruncher Let us go guzzle human beans!

The giants cheer their agreement

Childchewer Let us flushbunk to England!
Gizzardgulper England is a luctuous land and I is fancying a few nice little English chiddlers!

The giants cheer

Sophie Oh no!
BFG Shhh!
Meatdripper I is knowing where there is a gigglehouse for girls and I is guzzling myself full as a frothblower!
Fleshlumpeater And I knows a bogglebox for boys. All I has to do is reach in and grab myself a handful! English boys is tasting extra lickswishy!

The giants cheer

Bloodbottler Be following me . . . to England!

The giants cheer and freeze

The BFG and Sophie return inside the cave as the Lights cross-fade

Sophie It mustn't happen! We've got to stop them! We must chase after them and warn everyone in England they're coming!
BFG Redunculus and umpossible. They is going twice as fast as me and they is finishing their guzzle before we is halfway. Besides, I is *never* showing myself to human beans. I is telling you, they will be putting me in the zoo with all the jiggyraffes and cattypiddlers.
Sophie Nonsense.
BFG And they will be sending *you* straight back to the norphanage. Grown-up human beans is not famous for their kindnesses. They is all squifflerotters and grinksludgers.
Sophie That simply isn't true. Some of them are very kind indeed.
BFG Who? Name one.
Sophie The Queen of England. You can't call her a squifflerotter or a grinksludger.

BFG Well ...

Sophie I've got it! Listen, BFG, we'll go to the Queen and tell her about the *dreams*
    giants. She'll do something, I know she will.

BFG She will never be believing in giants.   *the giants*

Sophie (*with a sudden idea*) Then we'll make her *dream* about them. Can
    you make a person dream absolutely anything in the world?

BFG Well, yes, I could be mixing any such dream but ...

Sophie Then mix a dream fit for a Queen!

The BFG thinks, then springs into action

BFG Fit for a Queen!

*Exciting music as he leaps to his shelves, taking down jars, and pours small
amounts from them into one larger jar. He mixes the dream with a mechanical
whisk, then transfers it into a smaller jar. He puts it in his suitcase, grabs his
cloak and the "Sophie" doll*

He exits at speed

Sophie closes the "shelves door" as:

*The giants break their freeze and lumber up to the platform stage. The curtains
open and light pours in on the giants, who "rev" themselves up in formation*

Giants England!

All exit, menacingly

*The BFG enters, now wearing his cloak, and, silhouetted in the window,
starts running on the spot, carrying his suitcase and the "Sophie" doll*

Suddenly he turns, his back to the audience, and continues running

Sophie The BFG arrived in England. Sophie directed him to London. To
    Buckingham Palace!

*Slowly the back wall of the set flies out. Buckingham Palace, its windows lit
up, appears in glory upstage, as the BFG continues his progress towards it
and——*

The CURTAIN falls

ACT II

Sophie's attic playroom/bedroom. A little later

Family and friends are gathered round Sophie's birthday cake with lighted candles. The remains of the birthday tea are on a cloth, picnic-style on the floor

They all sing "Happy Birthday" to Sophie, and cheer and applaud

Mum Blow!

Encouraged by the others, Sophie takes a deep breath and blows out the candles. More cheering

Dad Make a wish!
Sophie I wish ...
Guy You're not supposed to tell us!
Sophie Why not? I wish ... we could start part two of the play!

Cheers and laughter. Preparations start and the tea things are cleared

Mum Do you need me? If not I'll do the washing-up.
Sophie Of course we need you! This is your big moment, Mum! (*She runs to the dressing-up box and brings back a cardboard crown*) You're the Queen! (*She puts the crown on Mum's head*)

All cheer and bow to Mum

Mum Well, I never! (*Queen voice*) It gives me great pleasure ...!

Laughter. Sophie helps her mother into a dressing gown

Sophie Right, you're in bed, asleep.

The bed is positioned

Mum (*getting into bed*) Oh. Don't I have anything to say?
Sophie Just wait, Mum. Ready everyone? Music!

Someone tinkles on the toy piano

Lights!

Someone lowers the lights

Mum (*springing up*) Hey, hang on!
Sophie What?
Mum Where's my corgi? I never sleep without my corgi!

Sophie grabs a soft toy animal and throws it to Mum

Sophie You'll have to make do with this. (*She steps forward*) The BFG, Act Two.

A child sounds a fanfare

Buckingham Palace.

The musical director takes over the music as the narration progresses

Carefully holding Sophie, the BFG crept along the back wall of the Palace, peering into the upstairs bedroom windows. Suddenly, through a crack in the curtains, they saw, in the moonlight, a sleeping face. A female face that Sophie had seen on stamps and coins and in the newspapers all her life.

A beam of light picks out the Queen's (Mum's) face

With great care, the BFG raised the Queen's bedroom window, and then . . .

The Lights come up on the curtains as, slowly, a giant-sized BFG trumpet slides through them, pointing towards the Queen, and a loud blowing sound is heard

Sophie climbs the steps to the platform stage. The trumpet recedes

Then the BFG placed Sophie inside the window, behind the curtains . . . (*She goes behind the curtains, with her head still in view*) . . . closed the window, and, waving goodbye and good luck to Sophie, strode into the garden and hid among the trees.

Sophie disappears behind the curtains

The other actors remaining now exit

After a pause, the Queen's head tosses from side to side as she dreams

Queen (*talking in her sleep*) Oh no! No! Don't! Someone stop them! Don't let them do it! It's horrible! Please stop them! It's ghastly! No! No! No!

As she drifts back to peaceful sleep, music suggests the passing of time, and lighting suggests the coming of dawn

There is a sudden knock on the door

Mary, the Queen's maid (Katherine), enters, carrying a tray with breakfast things and a newspaper. She is dressed in a complete maid's costume; from now on, all the characters are "real" rather than openly "acted" by the family and guests

Mary Good morning, your Majesty. Your early morning tea.

The Queen wakes up

Queen Oh Mary! I've just had the most frightful dream! It was awful!
Mary Oh, I *am* sorry, ma'am. But don't be distressed. You're awake now.

Queen I dreamt, Mary, that girls and boys were being snatched out of their beds at boarding-school and were being eaten by the most ghastly giants!

Mary pays attention

The giants were putting their arms in through the dormitory windows and plucking the children out with their fingers. It was all so ... so vivid, Mary. So real.

Mary has been staring in amazement. The crockery on the tray rattles

Mary! What is it?

Suddenly Mary drops the tray with a clatter

Mary!

Mary Sorry, your Majesty ...

Queen I think you'd better sit down at once. You're as white as a sheet.

Mary sits on the edge of the bed

You mustn't take it so hard, Mary, just because I've had an awful dream.

Mary That ... that isn't the reason, ma'am ... (*She reaches for the newspaper*) Look, ma'am! Look at the front page! The headlines!

Queen (*unfolding the newspaper*) Great Scott! (*She reads*) "Children vanish mysteriously from boarding-school beds. Bones found underneath dormitory windows!" (*She gasps as she scans the small print*) Oh, how ghastly! It's absolutely frightful! Those poor children!

Mary But ma'am ... don't you see, ma'am ...

Queen See what, Mary?

Mary Those children were taken away almost exactly as you dreamt it, ma'am.

Queen Not by giants, Mary.

Mary No ma'am. But the rest of it. You dreamt it and ... and ... and it's happened. For real! Ooh, it's spooky, ma'am. That's why I came over all queer.

Queen I'm coming over a bit queer myself, Mary.

Mary It gives me the shakes, ma'am, when something like this happens, it really does. (*She tidies up the tray*)

Queen I *did* dream about those children, Mary. It was clear as crystal.

Mary I'm sure you did, ma'am.

Queen (*lightening the mood*) I don't know how *giants* got into it. That was rubbish.

Mary Shall I draw the curtains, ma'am? Then we shall all feel better. It's a lovely day.

Queen Please do.

Mary ascends the platform stage and draws the curtains. Sophie is revealed

Mary Aaaaaaah!

Sophie looks frightened. The Queen looks frightened. Mary looks frightened, but recovers first

What in the name of heaven do you think you're doing in here?

Sophie Please, I . . . (*She looks beseechingly towards the Queen*)

Queen I don't believe it. I simply don't believe it.

Mary I'll take her out, ma'am, at once.

Queen (*sharply*) No, Mary, don't do that. Tell me, is there really a little girl in a nightie by the window, or am I still dreaming?

Mary You're wide awake, ma'am, and there's a little girl in a nightie by the window, though heaven only knows how she got there.

Queen (*remembering*) But I *know* how she got there. I dreamt that as well. A giant put her there.

Mary reacts with a gasp

Little girl, am I right?

Sophie Yes, your Majesty.

Mary Well, I'll be jiggered. It can't be true!

Queen And your name is . . . Sophie

Sophie goes to speak

Don't say it! Mary, come here.

Mary goes to the Queen

Her name is . . . (*She whispers in Mary's ear*)

Mary Impossible, ma'am, how could you know that? (*To Sophie*) What's your name, girl?

Sophie My name is Sophie.

Mary Aaaaaaah! (*She clutches her heart, looking, mouth open in amazement, from Sophie to the Queen and back again*)

Queen Told you. Come here, Sophie.

Sophie approaches

Sit down, dear.

Sophie sits on the Queen's bed

Are you real?

Sophie Yes, your Majesty.

Queen And did a giant really bring you here?

Sophie Oh yes, your Majesty. He's out there in the garden now.

Mary shudders

Queen Is he indeed? In the garden?

Sophie He's a *good* giant, your Majesty. The Big Friendly Giant. You needn't be frightened of him.   He's your best friend?

Queen I'm delighted to hear it.

Sophie He is my best friend.

Queen How nice.

Sophie Shall I call him for you?

Queen (*after a pause*) Very well.

Sophie runs to the window

Mary Is this wise, ma'am?
Queen Slippers, Mary.

Mary fetches them, as the Queen gets out of bed. She puts them on

Sophie (*calling from the window*) BFG! Her Majesty the Queen would like to see you.

Pause

Mary and the Queen look at each other, not really expecting anything to happen

→ **Queen** I don't see any giant.
~~**Sophie**~~ Please wait.
Mary Shall I take the girl away now, ma'am? *Q— No! There he is—the BFG!*

Sudden heavy footsteps echo from outside the window. Mary and the Queen look in fearful anticipation

The footsteps stop. A voice booms

BFG (*off*) Your Majester, I is your humbug servant.

Suddenly a huge puppet BFG head appears at the window

Mary screams "silently" and faints, unseen by the Queen X X X

Queen (*taking things in her stride*) We are very pleased to meet you. Mary, ask Mr Tibbs to prepare breakfast for our two visitors. In the ballroom, I fancy. (*Pause*) Mary? (*She turns to see Mary, flat out on the floor*) Oh.

Black-out, followed by scene change "blue wash" light

Regal music sounds, to accompany a transformation scene change

Mr Tibbs, the Butler (Guy), is found by a follow spot (optional). In butler fashion, he conducts the scene change, assisted by Mary and the Undermaid

Gradually the attic room disappears, as trucks revolve and the back wall flies out. The scene transforms into a ballroom, with high pillars and a red-carpeted staircase leading to an archway entrance. A breakfast table and two chairs are set to one side

When all is ready, Mr Tibbs signals for a royal fanfare and waits by the entrance. The Lights come up

The Queen enters in full rig—ballgown, sash and glittering crown, leading a real corgi

She is followed by Sophie, wearing the Queen's dressing gown, which is a little large for her

They descend the stairs

Mr Tibbs deferentially shows them to their table, and sits them down

Another fanfare is signalled by Mr Tibbs

He leads on a truck consisting of a grand piano topped by a chest of drawers, on which sits a huge BFG puppet, the arms of which are manipulated by Dad (a miniature version of the puppet). The puppet BFG's arms rest on a large tabletop supported by grandfather clocks as legs. (N.B. in the original production, Dad operated the giant puppet from inside; a radio microphone made his speech audible)

The music continues as Mr Tibbs summons an Undermaid (Rebecca)

She enters, in full uniform, and brings a breakfast tray to the Queen and Sophie, who start to mime eating

The Undermaid exits

Then Mr Tibbs fetches a stepladder, places it by the BFG's table, and summons Mary, who carries a very large breakfast tray with a giant mug and a heap of food

Mr Tibbs takes the tray and carefully climbs the stepladder, deposits the tray on the tabletop, then descends

The puppet BFG mimes eating

Mr Tibbs and Mary stand formally in the background as the music finishes

BFG By goggles, your Majester, this stuff is making snozzcumbers taste like swatchwallop.

Queen I beg your pardon?

Sophie He has never eaten anything except snozzcumbers before, your Majesty. They taste revolting.

Queen They don't seem to have stunted his growth!

BFG Where is the frobscottle, Majester?

Queen The *what*?

BFG Delumptious fizzy frobscottle! Everyone must be drinking it. Then we can all be whizzpopping happily together!

Queen What *does* he mean? What is whizzpopping?

Sophie Excuse me, your Majesty. (*She goes to the BFG*) BFG, there is no frobscottle here and whizzpopping is strictly forbidden.

BFG What? No whizzpopping? No glumptious music?

Sophie Absolutely not.

Queen If he wants to make music, please don't stop him.

Sophie It's not exactly music . . .

BFG Listen, I can whizzpop perfectly well *without* frobscottle if I is trying hard enough.

Sophie No! Don't! Please!

Queen When I'm up in Scotland, they play the bagpipes outside my window while I'm eating. (*To the BFG*) Do play something.

BFG I has her Majester's permission!

After a moment's concentration a very loud and long whizzpopper rents the air, causing the lighting to flicker and everyone to jump, then react

Whoopee! How's that, Majester?

Queen I think I prefer the bagpipes!

But she smiles, to Sophie's relief

Now, to business. Sophie, you have told me of your visit to Giant
Country and of the Giants' ghastly night-time children-eating raids. But
before we decide what is to be done, I must confirm the facts. Big Friendly
Giant, last night your ... er ... colleagues raided England. Where did
they go the night before?

BFG I think, Majester, they was galloping off to Sweden. They is liking the
Sweden sour taste.

Queen Right. Mr Tibbs, the telephone.

Mr Tibbs approaches with a portable telephone on a silver tray

Thank you. (*She presses the dialling buttons and waits*)

*A telephone rings. The lighting changes, staying on the Queen and coming up
on an area the other side of the stage*

*The Queen of Sweden (Rebecca), enters in full ceremonial dress. She holds
a telephone*

Queen of Sweden (*on the phone*) Hallo, Queen of Sweden here.

Queen Good morning, it's the Queen of England. Is everything all right in
Sweden?

Queen of Sweden Everything is terrible! Two nights ago, twenty six of my
loyal subjects disappeared. My whole country is in a panic!

Queen They were eaten by giants. Apparently they like the sweet and sour
taste of Swedes. So says the BFG.

Queen of Sweden I don't know *what* you're talking about. It's hardly a
joking matter when one's loyal subjects are being eaten like popcorn.

Queen They've eaten mine as well.

Queen of Sweden Who's *they*, for heaven's sake?

Queen Giants.

Queen of Sweden Look here, are you feeling all right?

Queen It's been a rough morning. First I had a horrid nightmare, then the
maid dropped my early morning tea and now I've a giant on the piano.

Queen of Sweden You need a doctor quick!

Queen I'll be all right. I must go now. Thanks for your help.

The Lights fade on the Queen of Sweden, who exits

The Queen hands the telephone back to Mr Tibbs

That proves it. Mr Tibbs, summon the Head of the Army and the Head of
the Airforce immediately.

Mr Tibbs bows, clicks his fingers and points to the entrance

Military music plays as, immediately, the Heads of the Army (Daniel) and

Air Force (Sam), in full military uniform, enter, carrying batons
They march in step down the stairs, not seeing the BFG. They arrive at the
Queen's table, stand to attention and salute

Queen Good morning, gentlemen.
Head of the Army What ho, your Majesty!
Head of the Air Force Toodle pip, your Majesty!
Queen We have a job for you.
Head of the Army Jolly good show, your Majesty!
Head of the Air Force Whizzo prang, your Majesty!
Queen Now, you've read about the disappearing children?
Head of the Army Jolly bad show, your Majesty.
Head of the Air Force Bally disgrace, your Majesty.
Queen They were eaten.
Head of the Army ⎱
Head of the Air Force ⎰ *(together; scandalized)* Eaten?
Queen By giants.

Pause

Head of the Army Hold fire, your Majesty.
Head of the Air Force Giants?
Head of the Army No such fellas, your Majesty.
Head of the Air Force Except in fairy tales.
Head of the Army Except in fairy tales.
Head of the Army ⎱
Head of the Air Force ⎰ *(together)* Ha, ha, ha, ha, ha!
Head of the Army Jolly good joke, your Majesty.
Head of the Air Force Not April the First, is it?
Head of the Army ⎱
Head of the Air Force ⎰ *(together)* Ha, ha, ha, ha, ha!
Queen Gentlemen, allow me to present the Big Friendly Giant. *(She*
  indicates behind them)

Head of the Army ⎞   Big Friendly Giant! Ha, ha, ha, ha, ha!
                      ⎟ *(together)* *(They turn. They see the BFG)*
Head of the Air Force ⎟   Aaaaaaaaaaah! *(They cling to each*
                      ⎠   *other in terror)*
BFG How is you doing, gentlebunglers?
Head of the Army ⎱
Head of the Air Force ⎰ *(together)* A giant!
Queen Indeed. Luckily a friendly one. His colleagues are not. Tonight those
  bloodthirsty brutes will be galloping off to gobble up another couple of
  dozen unfortunate wretches. They have to be stopped. Fast.
Head of the Army Message received, your Majesty!
Head of the Air Force Message understood, your Majesty!
Queen They must be brought back. Alive.
Head of the Army But how, your Majesty? I mean, giants . . .
Head of the Air Force They'd knock us down like ninepins!
Head of the Army Absolutely.

Head of the Air Force Absolutely.

Head of the Army Indisputably.

Head of the Air Force Indisputably.

BFG Wait! Keep your skirts on! I has the answer.

Queen Let him speak.

BFG Every afternoon all these giants is lying on the ground snoozling in the Land of Noddy.

Head of the Army Land of Noddy? What's he prattling about?

Sophie Land of Nod. Asleep. It's pretty obvious.

BFG All you has to do is creep up on them and tie them up.

Head of the Air Force But how do we get the brutes back here?

BFG You is having bellypoppers, is you not?

Head of the Air Force Are you being rude?

Sophie He means helicopters.

Head of the Air Force Then why doesn't he say so? Of course we have bellypoppers ... er, helicopters.

Queen Then, gentlemen, get cracking.

Head of the Army Yes, your Majesty. Forward!

Head of the Air Force Chocks away! Roger and out!

The Heads of the Army and Air Force turn inward and bump into each other

Black-out

The roar of helicopter engines echoes through the darkness, fading as a screen flies in for a shadow-puppet sequence, to music and sound

1) A bird flies happily from left towards right. Helicopter engine noises are in the distance. The bird sees something and squawks, flapping its wings and opening its beak in amazement

2) The BFG, running, enters from right towards left. He carries a tiny Sophie

BFG (*echoing*) Follow, follow!

The bird flies upward to avoid being hit by the BFG as he runs across the screen and disappears

3) The helicopter engine noises grow louder. The bird flies lower again, then has another shock. It squawks, flaps its wings and flies upwards, narrowly avoiding the entrance of three helicopters, one by one

The bird exits

4) The helicopters fly in formation, in a circular pattern. The helicopter engine noises fade to a background hum as voices are heard, as though through headphones

Head of the Army Where the devil are we going?

Head of the Air Force I haven't the foggiest idea. We've flown clear off the map!

Head of the Army Look! Look down!

Loud snoring noises sound over the hum of the helicopter engines

Giants!

Head of the Air Force Stand by, chaps!

5) Three soldiers slowly descend from the helicopters on ropes, eventually dropping behind the limit of the screen

The snoring continues

The colour on the screen changes to suggest the passage of time

Head of the Air Force Winch away!

6) The ropes rise, pulling up two giants each, trussed up, with the occasional moving limb. The soldiers are balanced on top

7) When all are visible, the voices of the giants are heard, and continue as the helicopters move off and exit, carrying their giant cargo

Fleshlumpeater I is flushbunkled!
Childchewer I is splitzwiggled!
Bonecruncher I is swogswalloped!
Meatdripper I is gunzleswiped!
Gizzardgulper I is slopgroggled!
Bloodbottler I is crodsquinkled!

8) The helicopter engine noises fade, as the BFG enters, bringing up the rear, carrying Sophie

BFG Sophie, we has diddly diddly done it!
Sophie Yes, BFG. We diddly diddly has!

They disappear and the lighting on the screen fades to black

Music plays as the screen flies out to reveal the attic playroom back to normal

Sophie, alone, is lit as she narrates

Sophie Meanwhile, back in England, a tremendous bustle and hustle was going on. Every earth-digger in the country had been brought in to dig a colossal hole in Regent's Park, near London Zoo, where the giants would be on view to the public. Ten thousand men and ten thousand machines worked ceaselessly through the night under powerful arc-lights. The hole was twice the size of a football field and the depth of fifty swimming pools. When the helicopters triumphantly arrived home, the giants were lowered into the hole.

The Lights come up on the giants, who, with a roar, tumble forward, DS of the platform, as though landing in the hole

The BFG watched the complicated operation, then peered down into the Giant-pit.

The BFG stands above, looking down at the giants

Fleshlumpeater Why is they putting us in this grobsludging hole?

BFG Because, Fleshlumpeater, here you is never eating human beans no more. From now on you is eating only these. Snozzcumbers! (*He throws some down*)

Giants (*in disgust*) Snozzcumbers!

BFG Oh yes! I is bringing snozzcumber plants from Giant Country and the Royal Gardener is growing them special for you.

Fleshlumpeater You is paying for this, runt. You is paying for this!

The other giants bellow threateningly

Sophie, carrying the "Sophie" doll, climbs the steps to the platform stage. She is met by the BFG

Sophie (*narrating*) That afternoon, the BFG brought Sophie to look at the giants.

The BFG lies down for a better view. Sophie manipulates the doll

The giants have gone to sleep—having their usual afternoon nap. They snore

BFG They is asleep, Sophie. You know, I is almost feeling sorry for them. (*He hangs his arm over the edge*) Now they is harmless.

Suddenly Fleshlumpeater leaps up and grabs the BFG's arm

Fleshlumpeater Harmless? I isn't harmless, runt! But you is going to be armless! (*He tries to pull the BFG into the pit*)

Sophie screams

BFG Aaah! Help! Help!

Fleshlumpeater roars as he struggles with the BFG, who appears to be losing the struggle

Fleshlumpeater You grobbly little grub! You is a traitor!

Suddenly Sophie pushes the "Sophie" doll perilously near the edge

Sophie (*with a shriek*) Let him go, you great bully, do you hear me? Let him go!

With a roar, Fleshlumpeater loosens his grasp on the BFG and grabs the "Sophie" doll. Sophie screams

Fleshlumpeater You squiggling, incy human bean. You has had it! I is eating you!

Sophie No, no! Help!

The BFG has recovered himself

BFG Sophie! No! (*He cries out*) What can I be doing? (*He has a sudden idea*) The trogglehumper!

In slow motion, Fleshlumpeater holds the "Sophie" doll high and steadily brings her towards his open mouth

Meanwhile, the BFG opens his suitcase and brings out the jar, glowing green. He pours its contents into his trumpet, and, just as the "Sophie" doll is about to be eaten, blows the trumpet towards Fleshlumpeater

The Lights snap to green as Fleshlumpeater freezes with a roar, at the same time throwing the "Sophie" doll up to the BFG, who catches her and gently cradles her

Fleshlumpeater, stunned, suddenly jerks his head from side to side, as the nightmare trogglehumper starts to take effect. He picks up a snozzcumber to protect himself

Fleshlumpeater Save me! It's Jack! It's the grueful, gruncious Jack! Jack is after me! Have mercy, Jack! Have mercy on this poor little giant! The beanstalk! He is coming at me with his terrible spikesticking beanstalk! Take it away! Don't hurt me, Jack! I is begging you!

He starts lashing out with the snozzcumber, which hits the other giants, waking them up. They pick up a snozzcumber each and, in unison, accompanied by angry roars, smash them three times onto the cowering Fleshlumpeater

All freeze. The BFG and Sophie pose triumphantly above

The Lights fade on the giants

The actors prepare for the final scene, removing their giant headdresses and collecting their puppets—Mum (Queen puppet), Guy (Mr Tibbs puppet), Daniel (Head of the Army puppet), Sam (Head of the Air Force puppet), Katherine (Mary puppet), Rebecca (Undermaid puppet)

Sophie (*narrating*) Sophie soon felt better, and, with the BFG, returned to Buckingham Palace.

Music plays as the cast assemble. The BFG remains on the platform stage, alongside Sophie and the "Sophie" doll

On stage level the others manipulate their puppets

The puppets "act" on the platform stage above, looking up at the BFG

Queen BFG, on behalf of England, on behalf of the whole world, we thank you, and gladly present you with the Queen's Medal for Gigantic Courage.

Cheers

The BFG stoops to collect his medal

BFG Thank you, Majester.
Queen To Sophie, too, we owe our gratitude, and announce that her orphanage has been closed and Mrs Clonkers dismissed.

Cheers

We invite Sophie and her orphan friends to live with us at Buckingham Palace.

Cheers

Sophie Thank you, your Majesty.

Queen BFG, we invite you to stay too, in a new wing of the palace, to be built specially for you.

Cheers

BFG Thank you, Majester. But no. I must be returning to Giant Country, to my wopsey cave and to my Dream-blowing.

Queen Very well, but you must visit us at least once a year. On Sophie's birthday.

BFG Majester, I will. (*He bows to her, then gently picks up the "Sophie" doll*) Goodbye, little Sophie. I is going to miss you.

Sophie Goodbye, dear BFG. I is going to miss you too.

The BFG kisses the "Sophie" doll, and returns her to Sophie. He puts on his cloak and picks up his suitcase

BFG Goodbye, human beans.

All Goodbye, BFG.

The BFG turns. The curtains open. Light pours through the window. The BFG walks on the spot in slow motion, his back to the audience

The puppets wave

The music builds

Black-out

FURNITURE AND PROPERTY LIST

ACT I

On stage: Colourful toys
Books
Dolls' house
Toy grand piano
Musical instruments including a trumpet/horn
Toy helicopters
Suitcase
Dressing-up chest
Rail of dressing-up clothes and masks, wigs, a crown etc.
Cuddly toys
Chest of drawers
Grandfather clock
Sophie's bed
Large studio window
Platform
Small staircases
Chairs
Banner. *On it:* "Happy Birthday, Sophie"
Unwrapped presents
Torch
"Sophie" doll
Nightie
Wall of bookshelves
BFG's cave. *In it:* rough-hewn table and chair, shelves covered with a
sack-cloth curtain, rows of glass jars, all flickering with different
coloured lights
Snozzcumber
Bottle of green liquid with bubbles going downwards
Five empty jars, one larger than the others
Fishing net
Telephone
Mechanical whisk

Off stage: Bath towel **(Daniel)**

Personal: **Daniel:** blindfold
Guy: birthday present. *In it:* copy of *The BFG* by Roald Dahl

ACT II

On stage: Birthday cake with lighted candles
Remains of a birthday tea
Cloth

                Giant trumpet and bubbles
                Slippers

Off stage: Tray with breakfast things and a newspaper **(Katherine)**

During the "blue wash" light following the Black-out on page 24

Strike: Attic playroom

Set: High pillars
                Red carpeted staircase
                Archway entrance
                Breakfast table
                Two chairs

Off stage: Truck. *On it:* grand piano topped by a chest of drawers, table made from
                four grandfather clocks and a tabletop and a giant BFG puppet
                Corgi **(Queen.** Optional)
                Tray with breakfast things **(Rebecca)**
                Stepladder **(Guy)**
                Very large breakfast tray **(Katherine)**
                Silver tray. *On it;* portable phone **(Guy)**

Personal: **Rebecca:** telephone
                Head of the Army: baton
                Head of the Air Force: baton
                Queen: medal
                BFG: snozzcumbers

LIGHTING PLOT

Practical fittings required: coloured lights in jars

ACT I. Afternoon

To open: Full general lighting

Cue 1	**Sophie:** "Music! Lights!" *Fade lights*	(Page 3)
Cue 2	The curtains are drawn, revealing the window *The area is filled with back light*	(Page 4)
Cue 3	The curtains close *Fade back light. Bring up lights on cave area*	(Page 4)
Cue 4	The BFG carries Sophie to the cave entrance *Bring up lights on the platform stage*	(Page 5)
Cue 5	They return inside the cave *Fade lights on the giants*	(Page 6)
Cue 6	Night-time music plays *Start to fade lights*	(Page 11)
Cue 7	**Sophie** "Goodnight BFG." *Fade lights on Sophie and the BFG. Bring up lights on the other giants*	(Page 12)
Cue 8	**All:** "Here we come!" *Strobe-type lighting effect*	(Page 12)
Cue 9	Eventually they stop *End of strobe*	(Page 12)
Cue 10	Music *Cross-fade from giants to cave*	(Page 12)
Cue 11	The **BFG** draws the sack-cloth curtain *Rows of glass jars flickering with different coloured lights*	(Page 12)
Cue 12	**Sophie** closes the "shelves door" and observes *Bring up lights on the platform stage*	(Page 13)
Cue 13	Swirls of mist envelop the stage *Coloured lights glow and dance on the mist*	(page 14)
Cue 14	The **BFG** transfers the dream to a jar and corks it *Jar lights up with a golden glow*	(Page 14)
Cue 15	The **BFG** transfers the dream to a jar and corks it *Jar glows pink*	(Page 14)

ACT II

To open: Full general lighting

Cue 35   A telephone rings   (Page 26)
            Bring up lights on another part of the stage

Cue 36   **Queen:** "Thanks for your help."   (Page 26)
            Fade lights on the Queen of Sweden

Cue 37   The **Heads of the Army** and the **Air Force** bump into each other   (Page 28)
            Black-out

Cue 38   Screen flies in   (Page 28)
            Bring up light on screen

Cue 39   Snoring continues   (Page 29)
            Change colour on the screen

Cue 40   The **BFG** and **Sophie** disappear   (Page 29)
            Fade lighting on the screen

Cue 41   The screen flies out to reveal the attic playroom   (Page 29)
            Spotlight on Sophie

Cue 42   **Sophie:** ". . . the giants were lowered in the hole."   (Page 29)
            Bring up lights on the giants

Cue 43   **Fleshlumpeater** freezes with a roar   (Page 31)
            Lights snap to green

Cue 44   The **BFG** and **Sophie** pose triumphantly   (Page 31)
            Fade lights on the giants

Cue 45   The curtains open   (Page 32)
            Light pours through the window

Cue 46   Music builds   (Page 32)
            Black-out

EFFECTS PLOT

Cue 1	The game starts again *Loud booming footsteps echo*	(Page 2)
Cue 2	The **BFG** begins slow, on-the-spot running *Howling wind blows*	(Page 4)
Cue 3	Ecstasy fills his face *Whizzpopper*	(Page 11)
Cue 4	**BFG:** "Whoopee!" *Whizzpopper*	(Page 11)
Cue 5	**BFG:** "Wheeee!" *Whizzpopper*	(Page 11)
Cue 6	**BFG:** "Just wait!" *Whizzpopper, followed by a succession of whizzpoppers*	(Page 11)
Cue 7	The **BFG** escapes through the door *Whistling wind, swirls of mist*	(Page 14)
Cue 8	**BFG:** "Where all dreams is beginning." *Electronic sounds to create a mysterious mood*	(Page 14)
Cue 9	The **BFG** disappears through the mist *Whistling wind*	(Page 14)
Cue 10	**Sam:** "... bit of algebra when suddenly ..." *Telephone rings*	(Page 16)
Cue 11	**Daniel** picks up the telephone receiver *Telephone stops ringing*	(Page 17)

ACT II

Cue 12	The **BFG**'s trumpet slides through the curtains *Loud blowing sound*	(Page 21)
Cue 13	**Mary:** "... the girl away now, ma'am?" *Heavy footsteps echo*	(Page 24)
Cue 14	**Mr Tibbs** signals *Fanfare*	(Page 24)
Cue 15	**Mr Tibbs** signals *Fanfare*	(Page 25)
Cue 16	After a moment's concentration *Whizzpopper*	(Page 25)

HEADDRESS DESIGNS FOR THE ORIGINAL
PRODUCTION
by SUSIE CAULCUTT

"BONECRUNCHER"

"CHILDCHEWER"

"MEATDRIPPER"

"GIZZARDGULPER"

"FLESHLUMPEATER"

"BLOODBOTTLER"

MADE AND PRINTED IN GREAT BRITAIN BY
LATIMER TREND & COMPANY LTD PLYMOUTH

MADE IN ENGLAND